Anonymous

Familiar essays, on interesting subjects

Anonymous

Familiar essays, on interesting subjects

ISBN/EAN: 9783337809751

Printed in Europe, USA, Canada, Australia, Japan

Cover: Foto ©ninafisch / pixelio.de

More available books at **www.hansebooks.com**

FAMILIAR ESSAYS,

ON

INTERESTING SUBJECTS.

' QUI CAPIT ILLE FACIT.' *HOR.*

L O N D O N:

PRINTED FOR LEIGH AND SOTHEBY,
YORK-STREET, COVENT-GARDEN.

M.DCC.LXXXVII.

TO THE

KING'S

MOST EXCELLENT

MAJESTY.

SIR,

IT is with the moſt humble ſubmiſſion that I dedicate, to the Father of his people, theſe Eſſays.

iv DEDICATION.

THE glare of Majesty has
not attracted me. Too obscure
in my situation ever to hope
that my name may reach your
royal ear; and partial, as I
may be, to the offspring of my
fancy; I am not sufficiently
vain, to think my book worthy
your serious attention.

To the *man*, Sir, I address
myself, and not to the monarch; and as I write profes-
fedly

fedly for the benefit of my fellow-creatures, could I have found a better hufband, a better father, or a more exemplary character, to *him*, let his fitua-tion have been what it would, I fhould have infcribed the Work.

THAT a life fo precious, fo invaluable, may be long pre-ferved, not only to blefs your amiable confort, and your royal

offspring,

offspring, but to give peace
and lasting happiness to your
people, is the most ardent pray-
er of

Your faithful subject,

and servant,

The AUTHOR.

PREFACE.

_____

PREFACE.

TO delineate the workings of the human mind, to develope the deep-laid schemes of the villain and the hypocrite ; to set up a light to enable the young and the unthinking to steer clear of the rocks by which they are ever surrounded ; to give them a chart, by which they may safely bend their course, and to mark on its surface the different points, where danger lurks unseen, where quickfands may interfect their deviating way ; this is, or ought to be, the motive

with

with which every man, who takes up the pen for the service of the public, should feel himself inspired.

When we look up to a Robertson and a Watson, when we peruse the classical pages of a Johnson, when we are acquainted with the pleasing style of a Goldsmith, &c. does it not appear presumption, in a young author, to attempt to wield the pen?

To the works of these men, indeed, this country is more indebted than they are well aware; and I am perfectly convinced, that their utility would be more extensive, were they read in our academies, as they would blend instruction and entertainment together. The pupil, induced by the pleasing recital, would find his manner of writing imperceptibly improve; and whilst, by these means, he became acquainted with some of the first personages

personages that ever appeared on the lite-
rary theatre of the world, and stored his
mind with the most valuable parts of history,
he would imbibe the style of the authors,
and, in a short time, clothe his ideas in a
dress more elegantly perfect, than he would
otherwise, perhaps, attain for many years to
come.

But while we advert to such great men
as these, let us not lose sight of many, who
have been brilliant ornaments in the humbler
walks of life. It is not alone the reciter of
the actions of kings and heroes, of the great
destroyers of the human species, who is wor-
thy of our notice, or who alone merits praise;
there are many who deserve highly of man-
kind, from their well-directed views; which,
though various in their efforts, yet verge to
the same point—the great cause of virtue.
This noble cause, whether defended by the

2   *short,*

short, but expressive essayist, who, like Mr. Vicesimus Knox, describes with accuracy, and by small detached pieces gives us, by intervals, every precept that can be wanted for the conduct of human life; or by a recital of living manners, such as we find in the works of the versatile Fielding, or in those of the all-comprehensive Richardson; in short, whatever be the instrument, by whatever vehicle the mental physic is conveyed, if the vessels are cleared from obstruction, and the habit restored to its original tone, the physician, who prescribes, is equally entitled to a reward for his time and trouble.

The writer of the present sheets, is the rector of an obscure country village; and has employed his leisure hours in sketching out different views of men and things, with this ardent wish, that should they prove be-

neath

neath the attention of men in the first walks of literature and science, yet to those, whose reading is not so extensive, and particularly to the youth of both sexes, they may operate in storing the mind with what is just and praise-worthy; that amusement and instruction being blended together, they may introduce the readers to a very intimate acquaintance with religion and virtue.

Emolument is by no means an object. Vanity can have no share, as the Author knows himself to be concealed behind an impenetrable mask: and, thus situated, he can safely declare, that the improvement of his fellow-creatures, and the most disinterested philanthropy alone, lead him forward to public notice. He would feel nobly gratified for his well-meant endeavors, could he ever know, that one young mind took a right bias,

3

bias, or avoided a deep-laid snare, by the perusal of what the author here most humbly presents to the public.

FAMILIAR

FAMILIAR ESSAYS.

ON METHOD.

WHERE lives the man who has not found the moſt beneficial effects from an attention to *methcd?* Let the ſtation of the individual be what it will, from the firſt duke, nay from the monarch on the throne down to the humble cottager, who goes forth in the morning to his labor and earns his bread by the ſweat of his brow; all, in this long-extended chain, either

feel

feel the good effects of *method*, or by a want of it, are perpetually embarraſſed both in time and circum-ſtances.

As I was ever partial to *method*, and have acquired habits of atten-tion, which I have found exceed-ingly uſeful, I have ſometimes, when in the company of the young, the gay, and the inconſiderate, made it the ſubject of converſation.

I was one day expatiating on my favorite topic to a beautiful and lively girl, who, as is too often the caſe with young ladies, from a flow of good ſpirits, and an abſence of care, was too animated, and too

volatile,

volatile, to trouble herself about any thing; and who often ftrewed the room, from end to end, with the various articles of her drefs, work, &c. I told her, that, would fhe but give fome little attention to *method*, fhe would find it of the moft wonderful ufe throughout life. She laughed at me for my anti-quated notions, and told me, that fhe even now found it fometimes impoffible to reach the parlour when the dinner-bell rang, and if every thing was to be put exactly in its place, fhe fhould never reach it at all.

As fhe poffeffed great good-na-ture, I preffed her to follow my di-

rections

rections for one week; viz. never
to leave any of her things out of
order, but to have a fixed place for
each of them. She promised com-
pliance, and perfisted with a perfe-
verance I little expected. For the
first day or two she found some dif-
ficulty, but it gradually wore off,
and, after the week was at an end,
she acknowledged that *method*, so
far from occasioning hurry, had a
contrary effect; and, as she posseff-
ed a good understanding, I am
happy to say, that, being now a
mother of a numerous family, every
part of it is managed with such regularity as ensures lasting satisfac-
tion both to herself and her hufband.

WAS

WAS I to write a volume upon this fubject, I could ftill bring forward inftances to recommend this falutary practice. Who ever faw a family well conducted where *method* was a ftranger? A friend of mine, who is a man of folid underftanding, has that peculiar attention to order amongft his domeftics, that, go when you will, you never fee the leaft buftle or confufion. All goes on like a well-conftructed piece of machinery. No bickering is heard amongft the fervants; becaufe their bufinefs is feparate, and want of employ never occafions interruption arifing from idlenefs. Go and ftay with my friend by the month together, and you never hear

B 3   him

him ſtorming at, or angry with, his
ſervants. He takes his uſual rounds
to ſee that all perform their reſpec-
tive duties, which are rigidly attended to, becauſe the neglect cannot eſcape the eye of the maſter.
Has he occaſion to rebuke, his ac-
cent is mild, yet firm ; uniformly
ſteady, and having judgment never
to find fault without reaſon, he is
implicitly obeyed.

To what then is he indebted for
the comforts he experiences in the
excellent plan he has adopted ?
Some will ſay, perhaps to his good
underſtanding and temper. This I
deny, for theſe alone could not produce the picture I have drawn. It
is

is *method*, that enables all his fervants to perform their work with fo much eafe to themfelves, and comfort to thofe around them : it is the common parent of uniformity and regularity, it has alfo amongft its offspring plan and confiftency, and wherever it appears diforder is banifhed, as it can no more exift where *method* prevails, than the hoar-froft on the bough, when the rays of the fun are confpicuous above the horizon.

I HAVE another friend, who is a good-natured, but a paffionate man (a very common character); the manners of whofe family form a ftriking contraft to the other.

B 4 PAY

PAY a morning vifit to this gentleman, and, nine times out of ten, although his eftablifhment is large, there is not one out of all his numerous fervants ready to announce you ; and you will ftand, perhaps, fhivering in the rain or cold, till at length, after hearing the parlour-bell ring for fome minutes violently, you are admitted by the fcullion in a greafy garb. My friend exhaufted by the oaths he has fworn, and the paffion he is in, and for which he begs your pardon, takes you by the hand, obferving, at the fame time, that no man was ever ferved by fuch a fet of d——d fcoundrels as he is ! and then vociferoufly cries out—Who's there ?

THE

THE butler now makes his appearance, and fays, ' Sir, you fent
' me to the poſt-houſe, and I am
' but this moment returned.'
' Where is William ?' ' Sir, you
' fent him to enquire after the
' health of Mrs. ———, who was
' brought-to-bed yeſterday.' ' Well,
' but where is the boy ?' ' Sir, he
' is gone to air the pointers, be-
' cauſe you fent the game-keeper
' out with the fick horſe to the
' farrier.' ' Well, well, leave the
' room.' Thus does my poor friend
for ever harrafs himſelf, injure his
temper, and diſtreſs all his intimates, when, could he be convinced of it, the fault is entirely
his own. It is the maſter of a family,

mily, who muſt pay a proper attention, and, if I may ſo term it,
do *his* duty, or he can never rea-
ſonably expeᴄt that his dependents,
were they ever ſo diſpoſed, ſhould
be able to do *theirs*, ſubjeᴄt, as thoſe
of my friend are, from morning till
night, to contradiᴄtory orders. I
could relate a thouſand inſtances of
the embarraſſments under which I
have ſeen him labor, for want of
that forecaſt and *method*, which are
ſo indubitably eſſential to a well-
regulated family. I remember din-
ing with him one day, when, by
his want of *method*, he had ſent his
butler and footman different ways,
his coachman was ill, and there re-
mained only the boy to wait, when,

unfortunately

unfortunately alſo, ſeveral gentlemen dropped in accidentally. Till
we entered the dining-parlour, he
never once recollected the circum-
ſtance, and was ſurprized not to
ſee the butler and footman in their
places; and I hope I ſhall never
ſit down again to ſuch a meal as
that of which I then partook. My
friend worked himſelf into one of
his unfortunate paſſions, for which
he begged our pardon, complain-
ing, poor man! of the infirmity of
his nature. Theſe circumſtances put
him out of conceit with his dinner,
although no man entertains more
hoſpitably or elegantly. This diſh
was badly cooked—that was over-
done — another was underdone —
in

in fhort, nothing could pleafe him; and his lady, who is a very amiable woman, and who was exceedingly hurt at his behaviour, attempting to foothe him (which, by the by, as it moftly does, only added fuel to the flame) he began to quarrel with her, and fhe left the table in tears. The cloth was foon removed. During the remainder of the afternoon, my friend, exhaufted by his paffion, hurt at, and afhamed of, his behaviour to his wife, in vain endeavored to force his fpirits into a temporary vivacity; and the whole company, inftead of enjoying the focial pleafures of the table with chearfulnefs, pleading fome excufe or other, took an early leave and departed.

I WAS

I was once told an anecdote of a captain of a man of war, who is an honor to the fervice, which fo pleafed me at the time, that I have ever remembered it. He was one day vifited by the captain of another fhip in the fame fleet; and, in the courfe of the vifit, his friend could not help remarking the readinefs and exactnefs with which all his commands were executed ; and, being what is called a good-natured eafy man (by no means calculated for a difciplinarian)——' Zounds, ' Dick,' fays he, ' how do you con ' trive to be obeyed fo readily, and ' with fo little trouble ? my d—n'd ' rafcals are fo perverfe, that I ' fometimes bawl till I am hoarfe,

' before

' before I can be attended to.' ' My
' good friend,' replied the other,
' the mighty fecret confifts only in
' this; I do *my* duty, and there-
' fore have reafon to expect that
' every fubordinate officer in the
' fhip does *his*; they all know that
' they cannot neglect their bufinefs
' without its being obferved by
' me; I never punifh an accidental
' or trifling fault, and I never over-
' look a great one.'

In commercial and mercantile
life, *method* is neceffary to its very
exiftence, as trade cannot be properly carried on without a very intimate acquaintance with it. It is
by *method*, and its appendages, order

der and regularity, that the tradef-
man, the merchant, and the banker
conduct bufinefs fo varied, fo complicated, and fo intricate. 'Never
' leave till to-morrow, what may
' be executed to-day,' is a very expreffive and comprehenfive adage.
Afcertain in the morning what is
to be your employment for the en-
fuing day; methodize your time
with a critical exactnefs ; portion
out every hour; adhere to your
plan, and, when you betake your-
felf to reft in the evening and lay
your head on your pillow, you cannot have a more pleafing fource of
fatisfaction, than to trace back the
routine of your employments, and
to reflect, that you have fpent the
day

7

day usefully; and, as a member of the community, have performed your part towards the public good.

SEE that regiment, how it moves! with what wonderful exactnefs does the whole body advance, or retire, at the word of command! See the manual exercife performed! Is it not almoft incredible to believe, that men, who perhaps, a year ago, followed the plough, and were comparatively unable to *walk*, who then had not one idea of the management of the mufquet, or of any movement to the found of the ' fpirit-ftirring drum,' or ' ear-' piercing fife,' now perform evolutions, that are furprifing to the

eye

eye of the obferver? *Method* con-
quers their almoft invincible habits
of rufticity. The drill-ferjeant, at
the ftated period, takes the recruits
into the field, and by *method* makes
the raw lad quit the roll in his gait,
contracted in the furrowed field;
and, in a fhort time, as Nature has
given him a good fhape and proper
limbs, you fee a fmart fellow erect
from the drill, and fo altered, that,
was he now to appear amongft his
former companions, there would be
few traces left by which they would
at firft recognife him. Happy would
it be, if corruption of morals did not
work quicker in the alteration of
his conduct, than the ferjeant's cane
in the improvement of his carriage!

C

By

B y *method*, the algebraift folves
the longeft problems; by *method*,
the mathematician climbs from the
fimple propofitions of·Euclid to the
Principia of our immortal Newton,
and all the abftrufe learning com-
prehended by the ingenious few.
By *method*, the laborious fchool-
mafter leads forward the pupils committed to his charge, and prepares
them for the different walks, to
which they are deftined in future
life. By *method*, the man who
has but a fcanty pittance of this
world's goods, avoids debts, and
brings up his children to earn their
bread, and to become ufeful·mem-
bers of fociety. And, by the want
of *method*, and of what is al-.

moft

moſt always a conſequence, the
want of *œconomy*, the moſt opulent peers are diſſipating their im-
menſe property; and ſome future
period may, perhaps, ſee their de-
ſcendants in abſolute want of *that*
which is ſquandered by them on
courtezans, race-horſes, or at the
gaming-table.

SHALL I ſay, as a clergyman,
that *method* is conducive to morality and religion ? Let not the au-
ſtere moraliſt condemn the maxim.
The man of *method* will ſet apart
a portion of his income for the relief of the poor and needy, which,
by aſcertaining his yearly expences,
he will be enabled to do; the man

of

of *method* is rarely a bad man; for he, who gives himfelf time to reflect upon, and to balance with precifion his *temporal* affairs, can hardly fail of cafting a thought upon *eternity*. He will therefore become religious by *method*, addrefs his maker with thankfulnefs, when he arifes invigorated in the morning, for his prefervation through the dangers of the night; and he will, from the fame caufe, bow before our heavenly Father in the evening, when he retires to reft, from a confcioufnefs of the unmerited favor of being preferved through the perils of the day, as well as for the bleffings he enjoys. By *method*, inftead of fpurring forward the almoft fainting

fainting poft-horfes, from the morning till the evening of the Sabbath
(blufh, ye mighty, at the profanation
of that day, now fo fafhionable, and
your breach of the decalogue!) he
will find time to attend to the duties of religion ; and, by appearing
at his parifh-church, aid the caufe
of virtue by the influence of his .
example. By *method* too, he will
always have his temporal affairs in
fuch order, that, whenever he may
be called away, a time which he
well knows muft be ever uncertain,
he may prevent confufion to thofe
he leaves behind.

T H U S have I proved the neceffity of *method*. We fee its confe-

C 3   quence,

quence, its utility, we fee its influence on the affairs of thofe, who
will fuffer themfelves to be guided
by its dictates. A want of it produces conftant hurry and confufion,
a diftracted ftate of mind and of cir-
cumftances, bankruptcy to the commercial part of mankind, irremediable diforder and ruin to profeffional
men and to the higher orders of the
ftate; whilft thofe, who are happy
enough to be in poffeffion of fuch
a treafure, or who are wife enough
to acquire it, fee their affairs profper,
and regularity eftablifhed in every
department under them, arifing from
fuch habits of reflection, as will enfure, not only prefent but everlaft-
ing felicity.

MEANNESS

THERE are few things of more confequence, in the education of youth, than their imbibing, in early life, that firmnefs of mind, which will lead them frankly to confefs a fault committed, even fhould they be certain that punifhment will be the confequence ; rather than, by mean evafion and daftardly fubterfuge, attempt to hide, what, perhaps, arofe from youthful levity alone, not from a bad head, or a vitiated heart.

C 4　　　HERE

HERE much depends upon the parent. Surely the boy, who, after being led into the commiffion of fome fault, or having accidentally broken or deftroyed fomething which he was forbidden to touch, comes with a noble, manly frame of mind, which is above deceit, yet with re-fpectful diffidence, and tells, in lan-guage at once fimple and affecting, the crime he has committed, or the accident that has befallen him, and entreats forgivenefs, is entitled ra-ther to reward than punifhment, and to the moft expreffive eulogium on his behaviour, accompanied with this friendly caution—*that you truft to his own reflections, upon the difa-greeable fenfations he has now drawn*

upon

*upcn himself, by his carelessness and
want of thought; and that for his
own sake, you hope he will, hereafter,
be more attentive.*

I WAS led into this train of thinking by some events, which I have
lately more particularly attended to,
and which prove what I have just
advanced pretty forcibly. The law-
yers hold it an excellence to be able
to state a case *in point*, and, as an
example from living characters often
works stronger upon the imagina-
tion than precept (however close
the argument is drawn) so I shall
likewise state, as counsel in the
cause of *ingenuousness*, a case *in
point*, so strong and weighty, as, I
hope,

hope, will entirely overturn a pof-
fibility of reply from my adverfa-
ries, who are retained in the behalf
of *meannefs*.

A GENTLEMAN, with whom I
have been long acquainted, who is
poffeffed of a good eftate, and is
really a refpectable character, was
bleffed with three children by his
lady, two fons and a daughter. In
domeftic affairs, and in the œconomy of her family, no woman could
acquit herfelf with more *eclat*, nor
with more addrefs and polite attention to her neighbours whom fhe
vifited. But, unfortunately for the
happinefs of herfelf and all her family, fhe had taken fuch a predi-
lection

lection in favor of Philip, the eldest son, that Harry, her second, who was two years younger, and Sophia, who was a year younger than him, often smarted for faults which Philip had committed, as he had it ever in his power to perfuade his fond mamma, that it was brother or fister who broke whatever was the caufe of enquiry; and no atteftation from the others, however true, had any effect to caufe the blame to fall upon the proper perfon.

I KNOW not how it happened, but the heir to the eftate, whether from the improper indulgence he received, or from fome inherent difference in his difpofition, had a remarkable

remarkable turn for mifchief, for evafion, and fubterfuge, by which means his brother or fifter were often feverely whipped for the tricks of their elder brother.

ONE day, in the fpring, when I was upon a vifit to my friend, and the children were playing in the garden, Philip contrived to run againft his brother fo violently, when near a very large cucumber-frame, that Harry fell backwards on the glafs, and, before he could recover himfelf, had deftroyed many of the panes; Harry, however, who was a lad of great fpirit, foon overtook Philip, and thrafhed his cowardly brother for his frolic.

I WAS

I was walking very near, in a clofe part of the garden, and, unobferved by the children, faw the whole tranfaction. The gardener, coming foon after to vifit his plants, and difcovering the accident, went immediately, to avoid blame to himfelf, and informed his mafter of it, adding, as the children had juft been there, he fuppofed they muft know fomething about it.

My friend, on this report, fent for the children into the ftudy: Philip came in blubbering and crying violently, conducted by his fond mamma, to whom he had related a ftory far from the truth, which fhe implicitly believed; and her rage increafed

creafed at the fight of Harry, who entered the room with that firm but apprehenfive look, which faid, *I know the partiality of my judges too well to hope for a fair trial, I have done myfelf juftice, and am prepared for the worft.* I had accompanied my friend into his ftudy; and although I had determined to vindicate my favorite Harry, yet I was likewife determined to be filent, till I faw how far interference was neceffary. Philip was interrogated, if he knew any thing about the cucumber-frame? When, raifing his fobbing face from his mother's bofom, he faid, ‘ that Harry broke ‘ the glafs, and that, becaufe he ‘ would not promife him to tell a ‘ ftory

' ftory about it, and fay the dog
' Cæfar ran over the frame and
' broke it, Harry had beaten him
' very fadly.' The mother now
again hugged her darling to her
breaft, and Harry was called upon
for his defence. ' Well, firrah,'
faid my friend (who, poor man!
was entirely governed by his wife)
' and did you dare to beat your el-
' der brother; and that too becaufe
' he would not tell lies for you?'
' Yes,' replied Harry, ' I did thrafh
' him, and fo I would again, if he
' ufed me as he does now; though
' not becaufe I want him to tell
' lies *for* me, but becaufe he tells
' lies *of* me; for he drove me back-
' wards upon the frame, by running
                              ' againft

' againſt me—for which I beat
' him.' The outcry was now vio-
lent, both from the heir and his
partial mother; Harry ſtood as if
he had too long been acquainted,
that he could not expect juſtice in
ſuch a court, and determined to
brave the puniſhment. The rod
· was called for, and an order immediately given, that he ſhould be
horſed on the footman's back.

I⊤ was now *my* turn to ſpeak;
I begged to be heard, and declared,
that l was cloſe by when the affair
happened, and that it exactly cor-
reſponded with the account which
Harry had given of it. This made
a material alteration, and juſtice
demanded

demanded that Philip fhould oc-
cupy the place which was intended
for Harry, whilft my hero received
fome warm praifes from his father.
And, to our no fmall furprife,
though but nine years old, he was
fo much affected on his brother's
account, that he entreated his father
to forgive him this once; adding,
that he himfelf had beaten him too
much, and was forry for it afterwards, and that *one* beating was
enough for *one* fault. I faw my
friend's eye gliften, in defiance of
partiality, whilft mine overflowed;
I clafped the dear boy to my bofom, told him no praife was too
much for him, and that I fhould
ever love him as long as I lived.

D   I fear

I fear I am too prolix. I have been witnefs to a thoufand other proofs of manly fpirit in the one, and meannefs in the other. The one, the darling of every fervant and dependant; the other, hated and defpifed. I once took the liberty of telling my friend, that time alone would convince him how wrong his conduct was in the education of his children, and that, whilft Harry would prove a bleffing to him, Philip would be ever a fource of un-eafinefs. I therefore now come to the circumftance which occafioned this recital; for I have juft heard that Philip, after being an idle, dif-folute, and extravagant fellow-commoner at Cambridge, has lately

9   fallen

fallen a facrifice at Venice to his numerous debaucheries, to the great grief of his fimply indulgent parents. Harry, my noble Harry, on the other hand, who was fent to the ftudy of the law, with rather a fcanty pittance, and told, that as a younger brother, his fortune muft depend upon himfelf, bids fair to be an ornament to the profeffion in which he has engaged. On the death of his brother, he was deeply affected, and never mentions poor Philip, as he calls him, but with the tendereft regard; and throws in excufes for his conduct, which nothing but the fincereft affection could invent. His father, now Harry is the heir to the family eftate, would

D 2 have

have perfuaded him to decline his profeſſion, but he could not accede to the propoſal; and ſays he ſhould be miſerable not to have his time employed, after the habits of induſtry he has contracted, and is reſolved to perſevere.

THE moral to be drawn from this recital is, I ſhould hope, too obvious to all my readers, to require any comment.

ON

ON THE PRESENT FASHION-ABLE MODE OF EDUCATING YOUNG LADIES.

THERE is no rock fo likely to be deftructive to my fair countrywomen, particularly the unmarried part of them, as the want of that maidenly referve, which heretofore was acknowledged by foreigners, as well as natives, to be fo peculiarly their due.

IN this particular we are indeed making hafty ftrides, and promife, in a fhort time, to vie with, if not go beyond, the utmoft efforts in re-

D 3   finement

finement of our more polished neighbours on the continent. Let us take a sketch of a modern young lady. It is by no means certain that she has the slightest idea of the superintendance of a family, or the management of domestic cares; and she would laugh in your face, were you to ask her if she ever undertook to make any pastry. But how does she spend her time? Perhaps she is better employed in works of taste, or of embroidery. To the common use of the needle I fear she is nearly as much a stranger, as to the performance of any domestic duty. But surely, Mr. Satirist, you will not deny her *books? there,* at least, she may seek refuge from

the

the gall of your pen. Oh! to be fure, if a new *novel* comes out, replete with modern fentiment, defcriptive of a young lady, who, from her extreme fenfibility, and unconquerable affection for the hero of the work, could not refufe his folicitations for a trip to Scotland, big with wonderful viciffitudes, taking care, however, that all fhould end happily at laft, and be palliated by the foothing idea, that, let the lady do what fhe will, her *fenfibility* is to be a full excufe—then, I will grant you, the hours will be fpent in the morning with *books*; and fhe will fkim the deftructive cream of fuch an author, with an avidity that is furprifing.

IF no work of this fort claims her attention, perhaps a walk with a female friend helps to kill thofe dull hours; and the walk is enlivened by the company of that fweet fellow the captain, or fome effenced puppy, who is quite accomplifhed in fuch kind of converfation as generally amufes the younger part of the fex.

LET not my fair countrywomen be offended, when I affirm, that not unfrequently, when I have met little parties of this kind, attended by men of the fword, in the Park, and other places of public refort, I have been at a lofs to diftinguifh whether they were women of virtue, or fome

of

of those frail and unfortunate females, who perhaps were at first betrayed by their great *sensibility*, and are at length become real objects of pity. I am myself a very reserved man, and have more than once been put to the blush, by that stare, that forward step, that vacant laugh, and that inattention to decorum, which mark the present race of females; and I have concluded them to be *demireps*, till some friend has, upon enquiry, undeceived me, when, although I was glad to find my mistake, yet have I grieved at the too near resemblance.

AT noon a hurry home to dress is usual; and the lady is then attended

tended by her hair-dreffer, who, for two hours, whilft he tortures her beautiful treffes into every fhape but that for which nature intended them, entertains her with the fcandal of the day; and often hangs over her in an attitude and drefs, the defcription of which alone would be indelicate; and if he is a handfome fellow, and has been long initiated into the myfteries of his art, I think the lady's virtue is in no fmall danger.

THIS, forfooth, is to be called improvement in our manners! I have often thought what wretched fools our great grandmothers muft have been, who, fo far from admitting

ting a diffolute, idle, impudent young dog of a hair-dreffer to their toilet, when they themfelves were in fuch a difhabille as muft give rife to improper defires in the man, were (poor fouls!) fo timid and apprehenfive, that they would hardly fuffer even a hufband to fee them without a cap.

But we will fuppofe the article of drefs adjufted, and the dinner difpatched. The reft of the night is fpent either at the play, the opera, the mafquerade, or at fome delicious rout, where the females of this enlightened age are early introduced into the deftructive art of gaming, which may bid fair to be the future

future ruin of fome *hated* hufband.

L E T me fketch the reverfe of
this picture, equally true, as I am
happy in knowing feveral young ladies, who have a juft claim to fit
for the portrait.

L E T me fuppofe a young lady
educated in fome diftant part of the
country, and far from the baneful
influence of the metropolis, whofe
father is able to give her a genteel
fortune, and with a mother quali-
fied and willing to fuperintend her
education. I will imagine her to
have been at fome neighbouring
fchool, to acquire thofe neceffary
accomplifh-

accomplifhments, mufic, French, dancing, &c.

I WILL conceive her to have kept good company, under the *eye* of her mother, and yet not fo timid as to make her afraid to anfwer a queftion from an agreeable man, though at the fame time poffeffed of that innate modefty and diffidence, that bafhful blufhing fweetnefs, which wins all beholders. I will not fuppofe her mind tainted by thofe books which preach up the uncontroulable influence of the paffions over morality and virtue; nor vitiated, as is too often the cafe, by the corrupting ftyle of the generality of novels to be found in

that

that convenient repofitory, a circu-
lating library! or by the inflamma-
tory converfation of thofe fafhionable
females, fuch as I have before defcribed.   And thus, ' bearing her
' blufhing honors thick upon her,'
her perfon remarkable, as to drefs,
in nothing but the *fimplex munditiis*
of Horace, not lofing fight of the
fafhion, but far from going beyond
it; her mind pure and uncorrupt-
ed, ftored with all thofe requifites
which make a good wife, and a
good mother; I appeal then to my
fellow - citizens, nay even to the
moft *abandoned libertine,* whether he
would not prefer, in his ferious mo-
ments of reflection, fuch a partner
in marriage, to the modern, fafhionable,

able, and accomplifhed female, with all her airs, affected graces, forwardnefs, unblufhing confidence, and fovereign contempt for every thing domeftic.

SUCH then is that amiable maiden, who, under the plaftic hand of a well-known female writer, eminent for her abilities, and her fincere attachment to the caufe of virtue, reforms the modern and fafhionable Florio.

I REMEMBER once being upon a journey, and arriving late in the evening at an inn in a country town, where the inhabitants were celebrating their annual affembly. There

There was no room where I could lodge but one, which adjoined to that in which fome young bucks were to enjoy themfelves, when the affembly was over. I went to bed late, but not to fleep; for the partition being thin, the noify jollity of my neighbours precluded all hopes of repofe. Their converfation turned upon the beauty and accomplifhments of their fair partners. To my great furprife, they ran over their different characters with fuch pointed remarks, and the features of each were fo ftrikingly pourtrayed, that I perfuaded myfelf I could almoft have identified the ladies, could I have feen them, by the defcriptions to which I was ear-witnefs.

witnefs : One was tall, but gawky;
another too fond of admiration ; a
third remarkable for her art, and
for her every movement being the
confequence of defign ; in fhort,
they went almoft through the room,
and fome farcafm or other was paffed
upon the greater part of the whole
fet : for although they allowed many
to be fine women, beautiful women,
&c. yet, from what I could learn,
even at a country affembly a hun-
dred miles from the metropolis, the
too great freedom of deportment
feemed to give general diflike. They
were joined, at length, by another
companion, who had been to wait
upon his partner home. An univerfal
clamour, the refult of envy, burft

E   forth.

forth. D—n it, Jack, cried one, how happy you have been! I never saw so bewitching a girl. All joined in the warmest eulogium upon *his* partner, and their praise originated from the very cause I have been, I hope, successfully pleading. Her blushing, unaffected smiles, her elegant neatness, and her innate modesty, won the hearts of the company, and they unanimously declared, that, could they obtain possession of such a prize, they should be infinitely more blessed than with any of those who had been successively the subject of their discourse; although they acknowledged several to exceed her in beauty.

LET

LET it not be faid, ladies, in your excufe (for excufe you cannot have) that the manners of the men fo far influence thofe of the female world, that the fault, if there is any, originated with them. Be it yours to reform that lordly fex; fhew, once or twice, your total abhorrence of the double *entendre*, your extreme averfion to the fmalleft tendency to a breach of the rules of true politenefs, and you ftrike the declaimer dumb. It is yours to guide and direct the turn of the converfation, and your tafk is by no means difficult. No *gentleman* will ever infult the ears of a modeft woman with the leaft indelicate fuggeftion, unlefs by the turn of

the

the lady's eye, or fome other certain prefages, he difcovers that it
will not be totally difagreeable to
her.

It is from you that our moft
lafting pleafures muft arife; it is
your own fault if you make them
tranfitory.

Too true is it, that the increafing
evil of feduction and proftitution
gives our fex fo eafy an accefs to the
indulgence of every criminal paffion,
that men feel great unwillingnefs
to encumber themfelves with the
care and expence of a family. But
the prefent mode of educating females, aids this caufe more than

people

people are aware of. For whilft men fee the other fex fo unac- quainted with domeftic and every valuable duty, tricked out merely to catch the eye, like the painted gingerbread on the chapman's ftall, and oftener upheld from frailty by *pride*, than by more praifeworthy motives, we cannot wonder at their diflike to a matrimonial connection.

It is to be feared, likewife, that the univerfal diffemination of no- vels, fraught with every delufive, yet captivating idea, and calculated to make the fair one melt, to ren- der her all nerve, and thus leave her an eafy prey to the artful and defigning villain, has added more

victims

victims to feduction, than any other caufe whatever.

LAY afide then, my fair friends, fuch confident affurance, and difgufting manners, in exchange for native innocence and unafpiring modefty; for rely upon it, that the former, fo far from creating efteem and regard, even in your warmeft admirers, will in the end generate contempt.

THE fops, and men of fafhion, will delight to trifle with you in an idle hour, but they will never venture a ftep farther. The fimple unaffected maiden, artlefs as the lifping infant, and adorned with native
virgin

virgin modesty alone, who shuns the public eye, and must be sought like the lily of the valley, will ever inspire the sincerest and most lively esteem ; whilst the artificial charms of the bold and forward, like the more gaudy colours of the tulip, although they may occasion a transient praise, yet will be soon forgotten, and leave no trace upon the mind, that they have ever been the subject of the slightest observation.

SECOND THOUGHTS ARE
BEST.

THERE is hardly a man living but would find, was he to turn his thoughts on this fubject, innumerable inftances wherein he would have been a gainer by an attention to the adage which is the fubject of this effay; than which no one is more common, even amongft the loweft orders of the people. In fhort, it is what every one talks about, though but few attend to and practife.

THE young, the gay, and the inconfiderate, would do well to engrave it on the tablet of their hearts.

I MUST confefs, that when I look back upon my former life, I can find numerous cafes wherein I fhould have avoided lofs of time and of money, trouble, anxious care, nay even fhame, had I but attended properly to this maxim, and given mature reflection an opportunity to come to my affiftance.

How many youths are there now fmarting under the confequences of precipitate folly (to adduce nothing worfe) who feel the truth of what I advance,

advance, and repine in vain at what they now fee, which, had they permitted themfelves to think twice, might with fo much eafe have been avoided?

T H E ftreets of the metropolis abound with numerous inftances to prove this fact, in thofe unhappy outcafts of fociety, who, had they well weighed the confequences of that fingle rafh ftep, which finks them for ever in the opinion of the world, might ftill have been a fource of comfort to their aged parents, whofe ' grey hairs they ' now bring down with forrow to ' the grave.' Alas! at the fame moment when juftice calls for ven-

geance

geance on their crimes, pity fteps in between the culprit and the aven- ger with fo mild an afpect, and pleads fo ftrongly for the wretched criminals, that the ftroke is with- held, and they are left to what is in itfelf punifhment fevere, the pangs of guilt, with its ufual ap- pendages, want and mifery.

Did the felf-willed youth, in his own opinion all-fufficient to the management of himfelf, and like the unbridled courfer above con- troul, give himfelf time for reflec- tion, he would then fee how indif- putably neceffary for his guidance through the mazes of this treacher- ous world, are the well-meant ad- monitions

monitions of his anxious parent.
He would then fee, that the refult
of a father's long experience is an
invaluable acquifition, calculated to
affift his own infufficiency and inexperience. He would then fee
(what obftinacy and weak pertinacity of opinion makes him blind to)
that *here* no motives actuate the
breaft of this his real friend, but
fuch as lead in the end to his welfare and profperity, fhould they at
prefent be unpalatable to his tafte.
He would then fee, that no envy, no
rivalfhip fubfifts (as among the affociates of his own age); but, on the
other hand, that the parent would
be happy to be himfelf excelled by
his fon, that every nerve is ftrained

for

for him alone, and that the father's greateſt and moſt ardent wiſh is to make him ultimately happy. He would then ſee, when he has loſt his indulgent parent, and reflection comes too late (not to his aſſiſtance but to his puniſhment) that the deſpiſing the admonitions, advice, expoſtulations, nay entreaties, of his father, will be for ever to him a ſource of diſquietude, which I can alone compare to the ' worm that ' dieth not, and to the conſuming ' fire which will never be quench- ' ed.'

IN trade, in that walk of life, where we find more phlegmatic characters than in any other, many a one a one has feen his name in the gazette, from fome rafh and precipitate ftep, which he could never afterwards retrieve, and which, had he attended to the adage I have chofen, might with eafe have been avoided, and his own life, together with that of a numerous family, have been profperous and happy.

How many married people do we behold dragging about a miferable exiftence, becoming plagues and torments to each other, who, had they well confidered the folemnity of the engagement into which they fo precipitately entered, and how unlikely their different difpofitions were to contribute to mutual comfort,

comfort, might have avoided that
mifery which they have entailed
upon themfelves for life?

MANY a man, who has been de-
coyed to a gaming-table, and there
initiated into that accurfed fcience
of play, has been led on, till in one
night he has ruined himfelf, an amiable partner, and a family, who had
the firft claim upon his property.
Could he have broken away, and
faid, he would confider of it till
the morrow, would he not, when
he awoke in the morning, and reflected on the gulf, into whofe abyfs
he was fo near falling, have lifted
up his eyes in fpeechlefs thankfulnefs, inftead of execrating himfelf,

his

his Maker, and all around him, at his precipitation and inexcufable folly ?

WHEN the brifk wine fparkles in the glafs, could the drunkard but reflect, that it leads to difeafes and the grave, he would furely de-cline the prefent jovial moment, to avoid future and irremediable mi-fery.

AND how many bigots to falfe honor do we fee in our places of public refort, who carry about with them that ' atra cura,' that corroding anguifh, which arifes from having taken away the life of another, and which no amufement, no diverfions,

in

in fhort, no invention of any kind can poffibly difpel? It muft ever line their couch with thorns, and make the bed of down to them more uneafy, and by far lefs defirable than that of Shakefpeare's celebrated cabin-boy.

How many victims to that dreadful crime of fuicide, tempted by fome fudden difguft or difappointment, fome fit of anger, or of caufelefs jealoufy (could they have reflected with coolnefs and temper on their fituation) might have been at this time alive and happy in themfelves; and at the fame time difpenfing felicity to their relatives and friends around them?

F   It

I T were endleſs to enumerate
the fatal conſequences of precipi-
tancy, or the many evils which are
ever ariſing from a neglect of the
ſalutary practice of reflection.

My young friends in particular
(and there are thouſands in the
world, who are paſt a ſtate of pu-
pillage, to whom the advice will be
of equal uſe) would do well, when
they are aſſailed by ſudden ſolicita-
tion of any kind, to give this eaſy
anſwer, which, like the ſpeech of
Shakeſpeare's clown, will ſerve for
almoſt every queſtion, ' I will con-
' ſider of it.' This will gain them
time, time will bring reflection to
their aid; and, I will venture to affirm,

firm, would they follow this useful precaution, they would, nineteen times out of twenty, escape the wily snares so often laid for youth and inexperience. To the volatile and gay such advice is more particularly addressed, the grave and serious being less likely to want counsel on this head ; but as the former class is, I fear, very numerous, wherein good health, great spirits, and an exemption from care, too often overbalance all the attention of the parent or the guardian, it is the part of the moralist to aid their work, and to throw his weight into that scale, which is too often overturned by vanity, thoughtlessness, and self-conceit. To the

F 2   incorrigible

incorrigible it would be in vain to addrefs myfelf; but, as I hope this clafs is not large, by the fame rule I truft there may be the more, upon whom this advice may not be loft; and when they confider that an attention to it will be productive of lafting and folid fatisfaction, as will the reverfe, of endlefs mifery, I hope they will learn to accept the one and refufe the other.

A CONTENTED MIND ONE OF THE GREATEST BLESSINGS PROVIDENCE CAN BESTOW.

IT is often a melancholy reflection, that, although Providence difpenfes its bleffings with fo bountiful a hand, we feldom find mankind contented with their fituations in life.

THERE is no fubject which has been more canvaffed than this among the claffics, and by Horace in particular; and in our own language, many are the authors who

F 3   have

have written ably upon it, with a
view to calm the difcontented, and
too often caufelefsly unhappy mind.
A great * writer, lately deceafed,
fays, ' that the aim of every author
' ought to be, either the making
' new difcoveries for the ufe and
' advantage of his fellow-creatures,
' or fetting well-known truths in a
' new and attractive light.'

THIS laft then I profefs to be
my wifh and defign, in hopes to
affift in allaying thofe felf-torment-
ing paffions, which find fo eafy an
accefs to the human heart.

WHERE lives the mortal, who,

* Dr. Johnfon.

did

did he fit down purpofely to find out caufes of difquiet, might not create abundant mifery for himfelf, and ever embitter his hours with unavailing anguifh ? For it is far from true, that our chiefeft mifery arifes from real pain and bodily difeafes.

SUPPOSE we *thefe* for a while non-exiftent, and yet what a nume-rous train remains, in the hypo-chondriac, the difappointed, and the envious! In fhort, it would exceed the bounds I have prefcribed to myfelf, accurately to delineate the whole group, which, having all the real comforts of life in poffeffion, are ftill undeferving of them, from that froward difcontent in which

F 4   they

they fo freely indulge themfelves.
I would have people of this clafs,
could I bring the powers of tranf-
migration to my aid, for a time removed into one of the more laborious ftations, and obliged to ftruggle with the difficulties which are
daily and hourly encountered in
them.

For inftance, I would have the
hypochondriac, who fours his mind
by the apprehenfion of imaginary
diftempers, for a time put into the
place of an honeft mechanic, who
has a numerous family to provide
for by the labour of his hands ; and
when, after having been fo long oc-
cupied in his new employment as

to

to work off the obftructions which a want of exercife too often occafions, he would be happy to return to his former ftation, of which he would then know the real bleffing, by hav-ing experienced the lofs of it.

ALAS! alas! would the com-plaining diffatisfied fons of plenty, inftead of looking upward and repining, that their lot has not fallen in a ftill fairer ground, and their own over-rated merits were not more amply rewarded; would they but look downwards, and fee the millions of their fellow-crea-tures pining under *real* want, *real* care, and *real* mifery, accompanied too often by excruciating pain and

incurable

incurable difeafe—could they be-hold even a tenth part of what the pooreft clafs in the metropolis and our great cities fuffer—fo far from nourifhing criminal, becaufe caufe-lefs, difcontent, they would lift up their hearts in thankfulnefs,' that their fituation is fo comfortable, their fubftantial happinefs fo great.

Did one half of mankind know what the other half endures, grati-tude for the bleffings enjoyed by the former, would infpire them with a fpirit of charity, by which the mi-feries of the latter would be greatly alleviated.

Sophronissa loft her parents when

when in early infancy, and devolved
to the care of a friend of her father,
whofe affiduity and tendernefs to
her could not be exceeded by that
of any one, except a parent. The
greateft part of her fortune was to
defcend to her on the death of a
diftant relation, and fhe waited fome
years, after her arrival at woman's
eftate, before that event took place.
When it happened, upon the inveftigation of fome writings, it appeared, that, from the neglect of
her father in executing fome law
concerns, the whole of Sophroniffa's
property was claimed by a ftranger;
and that, unlefs fhe engaged in a
law-fuit, which would moft likely
fwallow up the whole, there was no
profpect

prospect for her but of a total loss
of what was her chief dependance.

I n what a melancholy situation,
and how much an object of pity,
does Sophronissa appear under such
calamitous circumstances ! She was,
however, extricated from this dreadful embarrassment by a friend, who
found out, that the other claimant
was as averse to law as she could be,
and effected a compromise, which
secured to her such a share of her
property as provides her an income
fully answerable to moderate wishes.
What a source of joy and of exultation to all the true friends of
Sophronissa ! and, is it not to be
supposed that she must feel happy
indeed,

indeed, thus relieved from so painful a dilemma? Not so: she yet feeds unavailing disquiet; and, had not her friends been urgent, would have declined that compromise, which has ensured to her every real comfort. She pines after the enjoyment of what certainly was intended for her, but which, by an unfortunate train of occurrences, is totally out of her reach; and, though possessed of a good and much-improved understanding, amiable manners, and such universal good-nature, as renders her almost adored by her intimates, not only makes herself unhappy, but gives great pain to all those who are anxious for her welfare.

ETHELINDA,

ETHELINDA, on the other hand, was bred up in all the grandeur which wealth and opulence can beſtow. Her father was a courtier, and had a large income, ariſing from the places he poſſeſſed under government. Ethelinda was contracted to a noble ſuitor, and a few weeks would have ſeen her in poſſeſſion of a title, and of all thoſe ſplendid appendages which the world ſuppoſes ſo much conducive to happineſs. At this period, a fit of an apoplexy robbed her of her father, and, as his income depended chiefly on his places, and her ſuitor proved ſo mercenary as to have been attracted ſolely by the hope of emolument from the influence her fa-

ther

ther poffeffed, he took his leave with the moft cutting indifference. Ethelinda was obliged to retire, with her mother, to a fmall and obfcure village, on a fcanty pittance, which however they hufbanded fo as to be ever above want, and above obligation. Her mother, in a few years, followed her father. Grief, preying upon her conftitution, proved more than a match for a frame naturally weak. Ethelinda ftill lives admired and refpected by the few who have the pleafure of her acquaintance; though neglected and forgotten by the fair-weather friends who once flattered her in her life of grandeur. Yet Ethelinda never fends forth one murmur or complaint.

It

It is but seldom she will converse about her affairs, or chooses to unbosom herself. If she ever touches upon the subject, it is but to declare that she is perfectly contented, and much happier than she could have been, had she married the man who so meanly forsook her—that she is thankful to Providence, which saved her from the precipice down which she was so near falling—that she has learnt to contract her every wish into her present sphere—and that, when she looks abroad into the world, and sees thousands struggling with want and misery, it would be the highest ingratitude in her to be fretful and dissatisfied. Would to Heaven that those who pine in
plenty,

plenty, and murmur only for want of *real* afflictions, to bring them to a proper senfe of their duty, could take example by this fair maiden, and, without a tenth part of her excufe for complaint, learn to fet a proper value upon what they fo ungratefully poffefs!

Does it not appear that I have rambled far from my fubject? Mathematicians and philofophers fometimes attempt to prove the truth of what they have in hand, by fhowing what it is not; and thus, by holding up to my fellow mortals, I fear too true a picture of themfelves, I hope to eftablifh the truth of the principle I advanced, and to

G   perfuade

perfuade them to put it in practice.

I HAVE heard of a venerable
divine, eminent for his piety as well
as his abilities and learning, who
was grievoufly afflicted with thofe
two terrible maladies, the gout and
the ftone. His fufferings were long
and fevere, yet was he never heard
to murmur; and, when laboring
under the pangs of the gout, would
thank his Maker, that he was not
afflicted by the ftone; and, when
the excruciating pains of the ftone
were upon him, would lift up his
eyes in gratitude to his Maker, that
he had not the gout. Learn from
this good man, ye fons of unavailing

ing complaint, to eſtimate truly the
bleſſings ye have in poſſeſſion, leſt
Heaven, wearied by your ingratitude (to call it nothing worſe)
ſhould treat you as, Sacred Writ
informs us, he treated the favorite,
of the great Ahaſuerus.

FROM what has been advanced,
it may be fairly collected, that a
contented mind is *one of the greateſt
bleſſings Providence can beſtow* ; as a
want of it produces anxiety, ideal
pain, imaginary woe, with all that
diſquieting train of apprehenſions
and terrors which are the bane of
the comforts and bleſſings of this
life. The man who views things
through a proper medium, although

G 2   he

he fhould feel (as all muſt in this
world of care and ſorrow) his happineſs not quite compleat, yet,
when he ſees the good ſo far out-
weigh the evil, will thankfully enjoy what is given, nor repine at
what is wanting, ſo as to loſe the
reliſh for what he poſſeſſes;—whilſt
the envious, the diſappointed, and
the ungrateful, with all that numerous train, who baſk in the ſun-
ſhine of proſperity, are ſtill angry,
becauſe, now and then, a light cloud
overſhadows the diſk of the lumi-
nary. They are hardly ſo excuſable
in their behaviour as an infant who
rejects his play-things and accuſ-
tomed amuſements, becauſe his ever
watchful parents refuſe him ſome

6   improper

improper implement for fport, the poffeffion of which might occafion him much mifchief, and with which they well know it is not proper for him to be trufted.

THE LOVE OF PRAISE AND A SPIRIT OF EMULATION, IN YOUTH, MUCH MORE EFFICACIOUS THAN BODILY CORRECTION.

IT is of the greateſt conſequence, and ought to be the firſt object with thoſe who have the care of young people, whether parents, guardians, or ſchoolmaſters, to inſpire them with a ſpirit of emulation. Without this ſtimulus, youth will make but a flow progreſs, and, ſinking too often into a ſtate of apathy, will look upon the whole

plan

plan of their lives as mere drudgery, and then all hopes of excellence are at an end.

THERE is an ardor in young men, and a defire of meriting praife from thofe to whom they look up as the arbiters of their conduct, which, if increafed by gentle degrees, like the latent fpark amongft the embers, will at fome time arife to a flame; which, if properly managed, will produce fuch effects as muft enfure fuccefs, and make them, in all probability, fhining characters.

MANY a youth, timid, and apprehenfive, perhaps with nerves weak, from a fickly infancy, though

G 4   with

with good parts (were they properly called forth) has fhrunk under the chaftifing hand of an imperious pedagogue, and alfo under the repeated oppreffion and cruelty of his more healthy and hardened fchool-fellows; who, had he been placed in a private academy, where he could have been treated with tendernefs and humanity, would have made a rapid progrefs, and amply repaid the kindnefs with which he was indulged.

IT has been much difputed, by thofe who are certainly much more able to decide a queftion of fuch great importance than myfelf, whether more may not be done by fo-menting

menting a spirit of emulation · in youth, and bringing them to reflect for themselves, than by using one indiscriminate mode of corporal punishment for every offence.

I am happy in having some great men on my side, and therefore declare the more freely, that I have not a doubt but youth, in general, will make a more rapid progress under the man who studies their dispositions, and who, at the same time that he corrects the refractory, encourages and treats with parental indulgence the timid and the apprehensive.

I remember a melancholy instance,

ftance, particularly adapted to prove what I have advanced. I went to fchool under a mafter of fo irritable a temper, that the leaft offence was fure to incur bodily *correction*. There was one of my fchool-fellows whofe difpofition was remarkably timid, and his nerves wonderfully weak. This boy, from a conftant courfe of fevere *correction*, at length arrived at that melancholy ftate of mind, that he gave up all his ufual recreations and fports, and would fit, in a ftupid attitude, while the reft of his play-mates were enjoying themfelves; and when he has had a leffon to fay by heart to his mafter, although I have known him quite perfect before he went up to

repeat

repeat it (for not one of us took more pains) yet, when he began, so great was his apprehension, that he forgot every syllable ; and so much were his nerves affected, that, the leaves of the book being loose, I have seen them shake off, and lie spread on the floor, from his extreme agitation. I am sorry to add, that, although this boy by no means wanted natural abilities, a long course of improper severity made such an impression upon him, that he has never recovered from its effects.

I RECOLLECT also another case, of two lads, who, from constant flogging, were so hardened to all sense of pain and disgrace, that they
would,

would, at any time, for a fmall gratuity, take the fault, and the confequent correction, of another boy,
who was not fo courageous or fo
devoid of fhame.

If a lad's reflection cannot be
affected, by pointing out to him,
that he has a character to fupport,
and by treating him as if you really
thought him of fome confequence ;
if he is not infpired with a love of
praife and emulation, by pitting
him, if I may fo term it, againft his
comrades ; if, inftead of this, no
other method is thought of but
corporal punifhment for every offence, you blunt all thofe fine feelings, which might be made of fuch
infinite

infinite ufe in the formation of the man. You thereby render him callous to every degree of fhame, he becomes hardened againft your moft fanguine efforts, and is at length fent into the world with a mind but flightly improved; and his original boaft of a contempt for bodily pain, terminates in a like contempt for all kinds of mental fenfibility. Yet can I by no means ftand forth a candidate for that fort of indulgence which arifes from the fond partiality of a weak mother for an only fon. This is perhaps more baneful than the other, and leads to that ridiculous vanity, totally different from the love of praife, without which

no

no youth can ever make a good figure in the world. It is certainly true, that vanity will become the companion of that breaſt where ig- norance, puffed up by undeſerved applauſe, is alſo an inmate. The well-informed and cultivated mind, ſo far from boaſting of the progreſs already made, looks forward into the boundleſs tracts of ſcience, and, feeling its own diminutiveneſs, hum- bly recedes from public view. It is left for thoſe who know little, yet have been flattered into a great opi- nion of themſelves, who are vain from ignorance and ſelf-conceit, to court applauſe, and to become ul- timately devoted objects of ridicule.

5   Some

Some minds are more particularly
difpofed to vanity, the greater care
is therefore neceffary to damp fo
pernicious a paffion; and if ever
corporal punifhment may be admitted, it fhould be exercifed on
the proud and the oftentatious. To
thefe, an acquaintance with fhame
will be of ufe; whilft the timid re-
femble thofe tender exotics which,
fo long as the gardener nurfes with
care and attention, under cover of
the green-houfe, flourifh and profper; but fhould he ever wantonly
expofe them to the cutting blafts
of the ice-impregnate north, would
droop their tender heads, and no
longer expand their leaves, or add,
by

[96]

by look or odour, to the beautiful
appearance or balmy fragrance of
the fituation in which they are
placed.

ON

ON DOMESTIC PEACE AND HAPPINESS.

FROM the earlieft antiquity, writers, of almoft every denomination, have treated in exalted terms of the comforts of domeftic life; and the greateft heroes, ftatefmen, lawgivers, and politicians, have looked forward to the pleafures of their own fire-fide, as the ultimate reward of all their cares and anxieties.

CINCINNATUS, after commanding armies, returned with redoubled energy to the care of his humble

H   farm,

farm, and felt, I have no doubt, a degree of happiness, when seated with his family around him, far superior to any of which the most refined debauchee and voluptuary could ever form an idea.

It is in such a spot as this, that the man, no longer on the public theatre, but behind the scenes, unbends, and throws aside the cumbrous robe and ornaments he is too often obliged to wear. Here, enlivened by the prattle of his infants, and by the caresses of his amiable partner, he feels how great, how real, these blessings are, and how light, when put in the scale and weighed against them, are all those

7

thofe honors upon which the world,
the ambitious world, fets fo high a
value.

ˈI F, from the moft remote antiquity down to the prefent time, the
moralift, and the friend to virtue,
have enforced with the ftrongeft arguments the blifs of domeftic happinefs, to what are we to attribute
its declining influence over the manners of the prefent age ? I fear too
often to the improper indulgences
young men meet with from fimply
fond parents, and the great and eafy
indifference with which they indulge
themfelves in every grofs and criminal defire when they come for-
warder into life. Thus are the finer

fenfations

fenfations of the mind all blunted;
and, after becoming connected only
with the moft vile of the other fex,
they look up with abhorrence to a
connection with a beautiful and
chafte woman, dreading what they
term reftraint, and the reproofs of
virtue, too confcious of their own
acquired depravity.

Mr. Vicefimus Knox, who fo
ably, as well as learnedly, exercifes
the pen of a moralift and a fatirift,
inculcates in the ftrongeft terms the
utility, the good effects, nay the
neceffity, of early marriages. ' Dare
' to marry,' fays this writer, addref-
fing himfelf to the young man; and
his arguments on this head are too
good

good to receive any aid from what I might advance in fupport or cor-roboration of them.

But are there not other caufes, which eftrange our youth from that inclination they would otherwife en-tertain for domeftic enjoyments? In a former paper I have adduced one caufe, whofe influence, I fear, is too prevalent. But do our married couples evince their real fenfe of that peace and happinefs which I have defcribed as fo defirable? Here the reafoning, which the abandoned youth may bring forward, has but too much weight; for the contra-riety of tempers, the fullennefs of the hufband, the waywardnefs of

H 3 the

the wife, with the univerfal air of
difcontent, which too often charac-
terizes thofe who firft united with
all the ardor of love, and with vows
of eternal affection, aid the arguments of the profligate, and en-
courage that celibacy, which ftrikes
at the very vitals, the very exiftence
of the ftate.

But let not the libertine triumph.
Domeftic happinefs is ftill as defirable, is ftill to be acquired, and
ftill poffeffes all thofe real comforts
which have been defcribed fo often
and fo expreffively, both by the poet
and the hiftorian; and there are
many couples, to whom Thomfon's
animated defcription, in his Spring,
is

is fairly due. The critic, perhaps,
will call for an inftance to prove the
truth of my affertion. I have one
ready, and defy even malice itfelf
to contradict me. There is a pair,
who, in conjugal affection, long and
well-tried regard, and unfhaken attachment, for more than twenty
years, are indeed a model for the
imitation of all : who have raifed a
numerous progeny, and have omit-
ted nothing to render them objects
of admiration and efteem to all
around them. When I tell my
reader that thefe perfons are the
fovereigns of the ifland in which we
live, I feel a glow of exultation
that I am a fubject of fuch exemplary characters; who, amidft all

H 4 the

the temptations to which their fituation is more particularly expofed,
amidft all the glare of grandeur and
pageantry of ftate, feel happy to
refort from that burthenfome pomp
with which they are furrounded, to
the enjoyment of that privacy and
retirement which conftitute the very
domeftic peace and happinefs I am
delineating.

I T is with thofe, who following
a blind paffion, without once con-
fulting the fober dictates of reafon;
with thofe, who vifit that forge of
matrimony, *Gretna Green*, that the
caufes of difcontent too often arife.
I never, in all my obfervation, faw
three fuch Scottifh marriages turn

out

out happy. And why? Becaufe, had
it been confiftent with the wifhes of
thofe who have no intereft, but that
of their children, the journey would
have been unneceffary; and the
fame caufe which led the children
to act in defiance of parental au-
thority, will, when the paffions are
gratified, as certainly produce baneful effects to themfelves, the confequent refult of ill-judged meafures.

BUT the libertines will not con-
fine themfelves to thefe cafes: there
are many, fay they, where the parties came together with univerfal
confent, and with every profpect of
happinefs, in which the fame caufes
of

of diſſatisfaction likewiſe largely prevail. I acknowledge this with a ſigh ; having been often a witneſs of the truth of the argument : but the young man ſhould not therefore be diſcouraged from a voyage which he ought to take, but ſhould rather look upon thoſe quarrels, where he has had an opportunity of obſerving them, as lights and beacons, by the aſſiſtance of which he may avoid the ſands and ſunken rocks on which otherwiſe his veſſel might have foundered.

Too true, and melancholy to an obſerver of human nature, are the diſſenſions amongſt married people ; too true that they are big with

every

every bad effect to the rifing gene-
ration : and, what is more unfortunate, the remedy as often lies out
of the reach of all human help ; for
thefe overgrown children (for fuch
they are) having no one to whom
they can appeal, but beings poffeffed with the fame failings and infirmities as themfelves, are above
being guided by any one ; and both
fetting out wrong (yet firmly be-
lieving themfelves on the right fide
of the queftion) it is impoffible
but lafting evil muft follow fuch
proceedings.

WHAT then is the certain and
much to be lamented confequence
of all this ? It is becaufe we fee
daily

daily thofe, who, united with the fincereft attachment, are undermining by imperceptible degrees all affection, till at length they are as pre-eminently wretched as they were at firft pre-eminently happy; becaufe they lofe fight of that refpect, that delicacy of behaviour, and thofe little undefcribable attentions, which are abfolutely neceffary, as well after marriage as before, to keep alive thofe fenfations which were once their greateft boaft; but which, after confummation, are laid afide like a cloak, which is no longer of any ufe after performing the purpofe for which it was worn. For thefe wayward and wrongheaded couples—and there are few cities, towns, nay,

even

even villages, without some of them
—let us suppose in every such spot a
shrine established, like the oracle at
Delphos, with this addition, that
not only the prophecies, but the
juridical decisions, on every question
in litigation brought before it,
should be decided with infallibi-
lity.

To this shrine, then, I would
invite all these *passion-heated* and
passion-stirring couples to repair, and
at this tribunal bring to immediate
issue those quarrels, which, like Sir
Roger l'Estrange's fable of the larks
and the thrushes, might otherwise
be fomented (at least as an anni-
versary, if not oftener) to the day
of

of their deaths, and not only fo, but, by the continual addition of fuel, raife fuch a flame as nothing can ever extinguifh before the whole edifice is burnt to the ground.

WAS there an attendant on the fhrine, who was to be entitled only to a fmall gratification for each appeal to the oracle, I think he would foon become the richeft man in either the village, the town, or the city. The inconvenience he could experience, would be the exceffive fatigue of attendance, not only through the day but through the night; for his repofe would ever be difturbed by the clamorous appeals from curtain lectures hourly pre-
ferred

ferred to the oracle. Nay, I would
not anfwer for it but that fome, who
had been there, might quarrel on
their return, and again vifit the
fhrine before they could reach home.
A thoufand inftances might be adduced of the utility of this fuppofed
divinity: Such as where married
people are fo rude as to differ in
opinion before company (efpecially
fingle perfons) and, by appealing,
involve them in a ridiculous difpute; or, even if their children are
prefent, will endeavor to intereft
them in the caufe, wherein, by taking a decided part, they muft either
offend father or mother, or, by
filence, both. In all thefe cafes,
the fhort fentence of ' Go to the
                              ' oracle,'

' oracle,' would fettle the whole matter.

To fuch of my fellow-citizens who are married, and to their amiable partners, particularly thofe who fall under the above defcription, I now addrefs myfelf, and entreat that they will, by thinking more properly, prevent the pen of the fatirift, or the tongue of the libertine, from having it in its power thus to lafh thefe ferious though ridiculous foibles; remembering, that the firft and principal effort to prevent difputes, is, that each be more cautious in regard to their own expreffions and behaviour, and lefs agitated by thofe of their other felf.

I KNOW

I KNOW a very worthy and sen-
sible old lady, who has often re-
marked, in disputes between married people, that, let what will be
the contest, the victory belongs to
the party, which first quits the
field.

WOULD ye, my friends, consider,
that the quarrel most frequently
arises from some trifle, about which
both are equally indifferent; and
that it is only pertinacity of opinion, and blind self-willed nature,
which expects *too much*, and gives
too little, that protracts the dispute;
surely ye would blush from very
shame, and cease to wound each

I

other's

other's feelings, upon points as un-
important as a difpute between two
of your own infants about a top, or
fome other toy, found by one of
them, and claimed by the other.

It is a favorite maxim among the
ladies, that where married couples
difagree, the man has every advantage; as he can, if his home be
rendered difagreeable, leave it, and
by company and amufements compenfate the lofs he experiences at his
own fire-fide.

This I folemnly deny; nay, am
certain that the reverfe is the truth.
The hufband may indeed withdraw
himfelf

himfelf from home, and fhare in what will foon ceafe to prove amufe- ments, unlefs his mind be callous to every domeftic fenfation ; and thus he may for a while. wander from the tavern to the brothel ; but whenever he *quits home*, in *fearch of happinefs*, he may be affured that he will be as often difappointed.

LET thofe, who really poffefs the ineftimable bleffing of domeftic peace, value it as a jewel above all price.

LET not the drunkard, the liber- tine, or the gambler, ever laugh them (particularly the hufband) out

I 2   of

of their real blifs, to introduce them
to want, difeafe, and mifery.

Too often have the envenomed
fhafts of ridicule, conveyed, perhaps, in the epithets of Milkfop,
Jerry Sneak, Coward, and fuch expreffions as thefe, drawn away the
truly happy man from a fmiling,
and, if I may be allowed the expreffion, *paradifaical* fire-fide, never
more to return, till the dart, tipt
with the deadly poifon of guilt, has
been infixed in his bofom, and
which, perhaps, every effort of his
amiable partner could never afterwards extract. And you, ' ye fair
' married dames,' ever liften to this
one

one piece of advice, fo well enforced by the dramatic poet—let
your every nerve be ſtrained to
make home comfortable and engaging to your huſbands. Remember, he comes to you to unbend
from the weightier cares of life,
which furrow his brow, with a proſpect of providing for you and his
children. There are little peculia-
rities, perhaps, in which he places
ſome of his pleaſures: anticipate
that indulgence; nay, make it a
point of the firſt conſequence, that
he is never thwarted in ſuch inno-
cent recreations. There may be,
perhaps, diſhes to which he is partial: let them be often dreſſed with

I 3   your

your every attention; and, above all, drefs your countenance in fmiles, and let no trivial and accidental caufe of difquiet make that face lour with difcontent, which he expects, nay, has a right to expect, to behold adorned with chearfulnefs upon his return. Remember, the ftrongeft tie you can ever have upon your hufband, muft arife from unaffected and artlefs gaiety, which he is certain takes its rife from your fincere affection for him. It is not enough to gain your conqueft, unlefs you make ufe of thefe meafures to fecure it, A fmall part alone is done when you have obtained a hufband. The tafk remains to

10   keep

keep poffeffion; nor is it difficult, if you prove your regard by con-jugal fidelity, and a delicate and tender attachment. Let not love of admiration, or inherent vanity, or wayward wifhes of any kind, ever lead you to difplay a difpofi-tion, which may crofs your huf-band's views, or four his temper. Remember, and this remark is mu-tual, that the only way to be happy yourfelves, is to make each other happy: that, linked in an indiffo-luble chain, you will hereafter give an account at that tribunal where fubterfuge and hypocrify will not avail, whether ye have reciprocally fomented the fatisfaction, eafe, com-

fort,

fort, and happiness of each other, or, by the reverse, have become your own tormentors; and, what is worse, have, by example, entailed misery on your posterity.

ON THE CAUSES OF THE DEPOPU-
LATION OF THE COUNTRY.

TOO true it is, that the partiality for populous cities, and the refinements, without which mankind, in their prefent improved ftate, cannot even exift, tend very much to the depopulation of the country.

FROM the higheft to the loweft, this rage prevails; and, in my retired fituation, I have often had it objected by the fervants I have been in treaty with, that they, having

been

been ufed to a town, fhould be moped to death in fuch a folitude. All this, in every clafs, is a vitiated idea, and a falfe tafte, grafted upon principles which will not bear minute inveftigation.

THE man of fafhion, whether titled or not, quits the feat of his anceftors. The tufted lawn, the meandring ftream, the verdant grove, the gay parterre, with all the beautifully diverfified fcenery of wood and dale, are exchanged for the lefs healthful, though more enchanting, region of St. James's.

THERE, immerfed in fmoke, in noife, and diffipation, he no longer

longer feels a relifh for the beau-
ties of nature, for the mufic of the
fongfters on the bough, or for the
pleafures of retirement. Whirling
round in the vortex of fafhion, ftun-
ned by the buftle of the ' bufy hum
' of men,' he hears not the ' ftill
' fmall voice' of reflection, and often
neglects to think at all, till the turn
of the dice (more direful in effect
than the furious tempeft which
may perchance root up a fingle oak,
too ponderous to bear its own weight)
at once difmantles the woods and
the groves, and robs him for ever
of that feat heretofore, through a
long line of illuftrious anceftors,
the manfion of rural chearfulnefs and
hofpitality.

I s

I s not this then a falfe tafte? Can its principles be defended?—while the country languifhes under the lofs of thofe who are its natural guardians and protectors, from whom are expected ufeful improvements, productive of fuch effects as will provide the poor with bread, and. preferve them from their greateft bane, idlenefs, and, in the end, prove lafting advantages to the poffeffors, as well as ornaments to the face of the country.

How many fmall families are fupported by living in the neighbourhood of fome great man! Trade becomes brifk, and the faces of the inhabitants wear a continual fmile.

And

And if the *great* man fhould fortunately prove alfo a *good* man, he then brings neglected morality and religion into credit by his example and influence.

I f all thefe things are in the power of the great and opulent, do they not almoft wear the appearance of a duty ? and will not the wealthy hereafter be obliged to give an account, how they have difpofed of the talents committed to their care ? Are we not told, in an old-fafhioned book, that ' to whom ' much is given, of him much fhall ' be required ?'

A ND here let me pay the tribute

bute of gratitude to thee, my friend
from earlieft youth. Reader, were-
there many fuch characters, they
would refcue human nature from
the ftigma of that almoft univerfal
depravity which now prevails. Benevolus was the Squire of the village where I paffed my juvenile
days. He poffeffed a good eftate,
amply fufficient to have enabled
him to fhare in the diffipation of
the capital, had he been fo difpofed.
But Benevolus had fuch a partiality
for his native feat, that he feldom
left it. He was the idol of his
neighbours: he was the uniform
friend of the poor and needy: he
was a juft and upright magiftrate.
How have I heard the poor call
down

down bleffings on his head! and
yet the idle and the indolent were
ever certain of meeting with their
deferts. See him on a Sunday en-
ter the church (from which nothing
but ficknefs ever kept him) between
a double row of his tenants, faluting
him with the profoundeft refpect; his
ftep firm and manly—his exterior
noble and engaging—yet with fuch
humility thrown into his features,
which nothing but a knowledge
that he was then in the prefence
of the King of Kings could have
infpired. During the whole fervice
his deportment was devout, and a
model for thofe around him; which
has often put me in mind of Ad-
difon's Sir Roger de Coverly.—

Long

Long will the parifh mourn thy re-
moval, Benevolus; and, without
the leaft affront to thy fucceffor,
thy dependants will rarely, if ever,
again meet with fuch a guardian,
protector, and guide! How often
haft thou invited me to thy feftive
board, attended, as thy hofpitality
. ever was, by fobriety and decency!
How often didft thou call me to
affift at thy concerts, and taught my
young and unfkilful hand to form
thofe founds which have occafion-
ally become my folace through all
the chequered fcenes of life, even
to this very hour! Happy, happy
days, never half valued till more
weighty cares, more ferious occu-
pations, and the confequent remo-
val

val from the venerated fpot, have
taught me to prize, as they deferved,
fuch great bleffings.

ANOTHER caufe, ftill more de-
trimental, prevails, towards the depopulation of the country, than that
which I have mentioned : I mean
the demolition of fmall farms, by
laying them into large ones. Too
late, when the evil has obtained deep
root, may our governors deplore
that fome ftep was not taken to remedy this plan, fo deftructive to
population ; too late may the landed gentlemen lament their error,
by deftroying what may be fairly
deemed the very finews of the
ftate.

K   IT

IT would take fome time to fketch a part of the pernicious effects of this miftaken policy; to defcribe them all would exceed the bounds to which I have limited myfelf. Take one inftance, which will eftablifh the fact.

A GENTLEMAN has a large eftate round his country feat ; but, unfortunately, there are five or fix fmall farms in the parifh, which do not belong to him, and he is wretched, and not to be fatisfied, till he has purchafed them. The fteward is confulted, and, obfequious to the nod of his mafter, fets about it, and at length, by offering a great price, and by making the poffeffion

of

of their little eftates uneafy to the
owners, obtains the purchafe. He
informs his mafter of his fuccefs,
and tells him, that, however large
the price, he can enable him ftill to
make good intereft of his money,
which may be effected alone, by
letting all thefe farms to one of his
prefent tenants, whofe lands ap-
proximate, and who certainly can,
by making cottages of the houfes;—
or, what is ftill better, by their being
pulled down, and the expence of
repairs thus rendered unneceffary,
give a greater rent than the poor
but induftrious man, who has a
numerous family to maintain out of
the labours of his hands, and the
fmall ftock he is enabled to keep.

This

This, reader, I have been a witnefs to. I have feen the *great* tenant of the *great* man take poffeffion of the fmall farms; and, what is more, have feen the care-furrowed poor man, with his infant family, his weeping partner, with his little *all*, loaded on his only cart; his cows, his geefe, and his fwine, take a *long farewell* of that fpot on which the difconfo-late pair had fondly hoped, by mu-tual toil, to have fupported them-felves; and, by an early initiation to labour, have made their children ufeful, and, in their line, praife-worthy. I have feen the mufcles of the poor man's face convulfed with feelings too ftrong for concealment. But what muft be their future lot!

No

No other small farm is to be pro-
cured, so general is this destructive
plan! Some wretched cottage must
receive them, and perhaps, ultimately, the poor - house! Thus
they who, had they been continued
on their farm, would, by unceasing
toil, have contributed to defray the
burthens of the parish, would be
obliged to become pensioners themselves.

But much farther does the evil
extend. Was it to stop here, although pernicious in its conse-
quences to society, yet it would not
be so destructive, as in several re-
spects yet to be described; for some
young man, who by frugality had
saved a few pounds in service, and

K 3   who

who had connected himself with a maiden, equally prudent, might have ftept into one of thefe farms, and by fuch means have been enabled, without a crime, to enrich the country with inhabitants, by virtue of thofe natural propenfities we all poffefs. Take away from fuch the profpect of marrying and maintaining a wife and family, they lofe their fenfe of religion and morality, and look alone to chance fruition, till time difcovers the confequences, when the poor fellow leaves the fpot and flees, while the haplefs unwary girl, dreading fhame, and the ftruggle of providing fingly for her helplefs infant, ftrangles it at the birth. Direful, tremendous event! I appeal to the

moft

moſt learned in the annals of this country, whether theſe evils were ſo numerous when the number of ſmall farms was great, and held forth a proſpect of a comfortable home, where every honeſt deſire between the ſexes might be indulged. *Then* was there ſome inducement to the ſervant to be parſimonious in the expenditure of his money, becauſe he had this object invariably in view. *Now* the object has vaniſhed, the man is indifferent as to matrimony, and too often the alehouſe carries off all, or perhaps more than he has to ſpare, to the injury not only of his morals, but of his integrity.

How many broods of poultry, and how many litters of pigs, did each such little family rear up, and produce for fale, at the neareft town! whereas, now, the fatted ftately fteers alone (doomed for the London market) ftalk over the folitary and half-inhabited land. Mr. Paley, in his admirable work, fays, ' that in-' creafing population, and the num-' bers of the people, are the real ' riches of any ftate.' Every one muft acknowledge the juftnefs of the remark, which is well worthy of the attention of you, the natural guardians of the country, who pof-fefs landed eftates.

SURELY, if ever ye vifit your rural

rural feats, if ever ye take a circuit round your domains, the fmiling look of an infant peafantry, and the enlivening face of a populous, when compared with a folitary, country, would amply compenfate the diminution, which (if your defires are at all bounded) can be hardly felt in your income. I am told there is an act of parliament, which inflicts penalties on the holders of more than fuch a number of acres. Why then do the laws fleep? If it once was thought expedient to make fuch a law, I am certain it is equally fo to enforce it. And if our governors wifh to preferve a numerous peafantry, and ftop the corruption of morals, increafing

with

with rapid ftrides amongft the loweft ranks of the people, let them turn their thoughts to this fubject, and begin, at home, that reformation which can alone enfure *lafting* peace, and the means of *future fecurity* from *treacherous* foes, to this ftill happy and envied ifle.

ON EXERCISE AND TEM-
PERANCE.

TO the opulent, who are too often the indolent, few things are of more confequence than a due attention to exercife.

WHEN that memorable curfe was paffed upon our firft parents, ' In the fweat of thy face fhalt ' thou eat bread,' it alfo entailed a neceffity of exercife upon thofe, who, being by their fituation re- lieved from manual labour, would otherwife have been exempted from this

this univerſal ſentence. Even in paradiſe, where all things, but man's perverſe will, were perfect, labour was neceſſary; for we are told of our firſt parents, by the divine Milton, that

    ' Under a tuft of ſhade, that on a green
    ' Stood whiſp'ring ſoft, by a freſh foun-
      ' tain ſide
    ' They ſat them down ; and after no *more*
      ' *toil*
    ' Of their ſweet gard'ning labour, than
      ' ſuffic'd
    ' To *recommend cool zephyr*, and made *eaſe*
    ' More *eaſy, wholeſome thirſt* and *appetite*
    ' *More grateful*; to their ſupper fruits
      ' they fell.'

It is true, beyond a poſſibility of diſpute, that the human frame is ſo formed,

formed, that without some bodily exertion, obstructions of the almost innumerable vessels of our complicated system must follow; as in a well-constructed piece of machinery; if a stop is put to any one part, immediate confusion must arise, and the whole will be as certainly affected.

THOSE who are not obliged to earn their daily bread, must still find out some plan of exercise to carry off what would otherwise overload the vessels, when diseases must certainly follow; and they will, by indolence, become a prey to the gout, dropsy, apoplexy, and that numerous train of disorders from which

the

the poor and the laborious are almoſt univerſally exempted, and which find entrance to the bed of down only, and make all the elegancies of life taſteleſs and inſipid.

WHY has the brown cruſt of the poor man ever been deſcribed as eaten with ſo peculiar a reliſh? It is becauſe labour has given him that appetite, for which the epicure in vain ſeeks amongſt high-ſeaſoned diſhes, and the almoſt countleſs variety with which his table is loaded. How many conſtitutions experience a premature decay, from thoſe two direful foes to man, indolence and intemperance!

'EAT

'EAT to live, and not live to
' eat,' fhould be fixed in capital let-
ters at the fummit of the towering
epargne; or repeated by an attendant, fimilar to him who was ap-
pointed daily to remind the king his
mafter that he muft die.

WAS this admonition properly
attended to, we fhould not fee fo
many pallid countenances, and fwoln
bodies, burthened with the effects of
indigeftion.

. IT is a maxim of long ftanding,
that every man is either a fool, or
his own phyfician, at forty. Was
I to attempt an application of this
adage, it would, I fear, bear hard

6   upon

upon fo large a fhare of my fellow-citizens, that I will not apply it. But as all mankind have an inftinctive attachment to this life, wifely implanted by the author of our exiftence, for good and juft pur-pofes, how ftrange is it, that our appetites and paffions, joined to the enflaving force of habit, fhould fo overpower what we all know to be right, as to engage us in a plan moft certainly deftructive to that very exiftence to which we cling, like the finking mariner to the wreck, with fuch extreme tenacity!

WERE the rules of temperance and exercife duly attended to, the drugs in the apothecary's fhop would

lie

lie ufelefs : and energy, activity, and
a brifk flow of fpirits, would cha-
racterife thofe, who now feel only· a
temporary relief from pain, by the
affiftance of that art, which would
then be chiefly confined to accidental diforders, from which none
can promife themfelves fecurity, and
which make indeed but a very fmall
part of the emoluments of the phy-
fical tribe.

LET it not, however, be thought
·that I intend the fmalleft farcafm on
thofe, whofe profeffion I venerate
very highly, and who ought, as they
defervedly do, to ftand in the moft
exalted fphere in the opinion of
their fellow-creatures. Where fhall
we find a defcription of this clafs

L   equal

equal to that given us by the juftly
admired writer, Mr. Crabbe, in his
Library? and which I beg leave to
quote, as a tribute due to fo valuable a part of fociety:

‘ There Phyfic fills the fpace, and far
‘ around,
‘ Pile above pile, her learned works abound,
‘ Glorious their aim—to aid the labouring
‘ heart;
‘ To war with death, and ftop his flying
‘ dart;
‘ To trace the fource from whence the
‘ conteft grew,
‘ And life’s fhort leafe on eafier terms re-
‘ new;
‘ To calm the frenzy of the burning brain;
‘ To heal the tortures of imploring pain;
‘ Or, when more powerful ills all efforts
‘ brave,
‘ To eafe the victim, no device can fave,
‘ And fmooth the ftormy paffage to the
‘ grave.’

THE

THE habitual drunkard makes quick approaches to that ' bourn ' from which no traveller returns,' and brings on, too often, that confuming malady, which (flattering only to its prey) deftroys the lungs, and waftes the human frame by imperceptible degrees. But how few, could the numbers be afcertained, fall a facrifice to this vice, compared to thofe who look down with horror on fuch characters as thefe, and yet are equally culpable, by not reftraining a kindred appetite in the article of eating!

THE dignitary in the church, lolling on his velvet cufhion, under the pealing organ, and who would

L 2   fhudder

fhudder at the idea of abfolute inebriety, yet thinks with glee of the
delicacies which await him when
church is over, and the table co-
vered for dinner.

THE bodies corporate of our populous cities have long been a ftanding jeft of the witlings and the ca-
ricaturifts of the age. To me .the
difference is not fo great as fome
may imagine, whether the body is
undermined by inebriety, attended
by its conftant companion, derange-
ment of the mental faculties, or
whether it is equally weakened by a
load of .indigefted food piled up in
the ftomach, which, although it does
not produce the madnefs and dif-
traction

traction which wine and ftrong drink occafion, yet oppreffes the foul with fuch a. weight, that the man, with his eyes fet, and panting for breath under his ponderous burthen, becomes little better than merely an animal. In one refpect the animal is the better character, for the brute creation know when they have e-nough, and feldom overgorge themfelves, but lie down fatisfied with what nature requires.

COULD men be perfuaded to rife from the pleafures of the table with an appetite, they would find fo. much comfort, that, when they took into the fcale, how much they, by this means, contributed to lon-

gevity,

gevity, I should suppose no gratification of the palate could counterbalance the advantages. To this let there be added such hours as Nature intended for rest, and, instead of consuming the night in company, and sleeping out the best part of the day, be advised to retire early to repose, and with the plowman in the morning, listen to the early serenade of the lark. Calculation has proved how many years would, by these means, be added to a man's waking existence. Should the sons of feasting plead, that it would be in vain to attempt to leave off customs to which they have been so long habituated, let them recollect the remarkable instance

ſtance of that noble Venetian Lewis
Cornaro, who, with a bad conſtitu-
tion, weakened by repeated exceſs,
began a reformation at forty years
of age, and, by perſeverance in a
plan of temperance and exerciſe,
lived to be a very old man; which
proves at once, that it is poſſible to
diſcontinue them, inveterate as they
may be, and burſt the chains, however maſſy, by which we ſuffer our-
ſelves to be bound.

YET will the epicure ſtill feaſt,
and the dignitary ſtill reckon upon
his delicacies; and the different of-
ficers of the bodies corporate ſtill
enjoy their turtle and their veniſon.
Still will the night be waſted in

com-

company; and the morning, fo often fung and celebrated both by
ancient and modern authors, be
dozed away in fleep and infenfi-
bility; and my antiquated and ruf-
ticated notions be treated with dif-
dain. Well, then, if it muft be fo,
I can only heave a figh of pity for
my fellow-creatures; ftill confcious,
whilft truth remains afcertainable,
that the beft of the argument is on
my fide; begging only, that ye,
who, like fuicides (pardon the expreffion) are carelefs of the true
means of prolonging your exiftence,
and who may be called galley-flaves,
chained to the oar of your appetites
and paffions, would believe the motive which actuated the writer to be
that

that of the moſt unfeigned regard
for your welfare, with the hope,
though perhaps a vain hope, that
in ſome inſtances the admonitions,
here imparted, may have their due
and proper effeſt.

ON HUMANITY TO ANIMALS.

IT is of the firſt conſequence, in training up the youth of both ſexes, that they be early inſpired with humanity, and particularly that its principles be implanted ſtrongly in their yet tender hearts, to guard them againſt inflicting wanton pain on thoſe animals, which uſe or accident may occaſionally put into their power.

How many diſpoſitions have been formed to cruelty, from being permitted to tear off the wings of flies, whipping

whipping cats and dogs, or tying a
string to the leg of a bird, and twirl-
ing it round till the thigh is torn
from · the bleeding body ! How
highly neceffary is it for parents to
watch with anxious care over their
offspring, and ftrenuoufly to op-
pofe fuch habits as thefe (though
they often arife from mere childifh
imitations, rather than from a bad
heart) and to ftifle in the birth
every wifh and defire to inflict torture, or even give unneceffary pain !

I HAVE feen one inftance to the
contrary. It was of an amiable
young lady, with whom fuch care
was taken to keep her fenfibility
awake, that fhe was in a continual
agitation,

agitation, by thofe unavoidable ac-
cidents which animals experience ;
but this fo rarely happens, that the
danger lies on the other fide, and
there is little fear of fuch a quality
being carried too far. This tendency to cruelty, fo direful in its
effects to young minds, ' grows with
' their growth, and ftrengthens with
' their ftrength,' till, by the time
boys arrive at manhood, they have
loft all thofe fenfitive perceptions,
which do honor to human nature.
Young mafter muft have a little
horfe to ride, and a favorite fpaniel
to accompany him ; thefe alter-
nately commit, what he terms faults,
and, becaufe they are his, he is to
chaftife them as he thinks proper.

If

If the young gentleman is heir to a
good eftate, the domeftics look up
to him as their future mafter, and,
not daring to difpleafe him, he is
foon initiated by the fervants into
the ' art of ingenioufly tormenting'
all forts of animals, fuch as tying
cats together by their tails, which
irritates them to fight, or by fhoe-
ing them with walnut-fhells; an
owl is to be attached to the back of
a duck, which of courfe dives in
hopes of exonerating itfelf, and the
owl follows, and when both return
to the furface, the wet, but tor-
tured owl, affords wonderful fatif-
faction to the young fquire and his
affociates. Badger-baiting is fucceeded by bull-baiting, and our

hero

hero is at length ufhered into that noble diverfion, the folace of fome of our nobility, yet the difgrace of this kingdom, the cock-pit, where, amidft dreadful oaths and execrations, he compleats a character which is above all fear of fhame or humanity. He is fo well taught to laugh at the diftreffes and infirmities of his fellow-creatures, that he would look upon it as a glorious act to drive over an old woman, fhould fhe happen to be too decrepit to efcape the career of his phaeton; and his fupreme delight is to fee two human beings expofed naked upon a ftage, and ufing the moft fkilful efforts to knock each other on the head. What a fhout rends

the air, when one has laid his anta-
gonift, for a time, breathlefs on the
ftage, with the blood ftreaming
from the wound! In vain do we,
who are not initiated into the fupreme felicity of fuch fcenes, look
around to find out that pleafure of
which we can form no idea. But
furely, amongft the fofter difpofitions of the other fex, we fhall never
find the leaft tendency to cruelty.
Yet are the ladies of this ifland not
exempt, although I am proud to
boaft, that there are no women in
the known world, who poffefs fo
much delicacy and fenfibility; and
yet, in fome inftances, I cannot ex-
culpate them. Do they not con-
fine the feathered warblers in a
cage,

cage, barring them from freedom, their inherent right, and from those employments to which inftinctive nature fo ftrongly impels them? Will the lark carol with that energy, on one poor fod in his wire prifon, as when he foars into the fky till his flight is imperceptible? I have known feveral of my female friends ambitious of a curious collection of infects. What was the confequence? In the courfe of the fummer you fee their dreffing-rooms adorned with a number of thofe beautiful flutterers, ftuck through with large pins; and I have feen my fair friends exulting in having caught one with variegated colours, holding his wings after he was impaled, left

the

the agonies of expiring life fhould injure his beauty after death. Is the lady fond of angling? fhe takes her ftation by the fide of the murmuring ftream, and, with the utmoft unconcern, forces the barbed hook through the defencelefs body of the writhing worm, and there it muft remain, in torture, as a bait for the fifh ; for, fhould death put a period to its exiftence, it is no longer fit for ufe, and muft be fucceeded by another fufferer. Can there be a more dreadful, a more ingenious piece of torture contrived than this? yet will they tell you, with a laugh, it is only a worm. Is pain then confined to beings of a larger bulk ? Has not the worm a

M   body,

body, in all its parts exquifitely formed by the hand of Providence ? Shakefpeare fays,

———' Whilft the poor worm, which we
' tread upon,
' In corporal fuff'rance feels a pang as
' great
' As when a giant dies.'

IT is furely unpleafant to reflect, that there are hardly any of thofe fports which gentlemen purfue, but are purchafed at the expence of fome animal or another. The hawk flies at the trembling pigeon ; the quick-fcented hound purfues the timid hare through all her doubles ; the pointer, with inflated noftril, finds the partridge in the ftubble, and

man

man muſt be gratified by nothing leſs than the death of the animals ſubmitted to his will. The race-horſe ſtrains his every muſcle, ever to torment, and fleets over the courſe with a ſpeed almoſt incredible; but his aſtoniſhing ſwiftneſs is of no uſe to the ſober part of mankind. The ſums allowed by our former ſovereigns, granted from a wiſe motive, to improve the breed of horſes, no longer are ex-pended with that view; but, on the other hand, to train up an expen-ſive breed, calculated only to ruin thoſe who have not been initiated into the myſteries of the turf. Whilſt the animals themſelves, kept in an unnatural ſtate, inſtead of ranging

abroad

abroad in the fields, pafs a ufelefs exiſtence, and are kept in health by phyſic, and by periodical returns of exercife, the only employment for boys, brought up in wickednefs, and idlenefs, and gaming.

THERE is another fpecies of in-humanity, which all ranks, except the poor and indigent, ſtand accuſed of:—This is the cuſtom of travelling poſt. How have I feen the trembling chaife-horfe panting for breath, every limb ſhattered by the hardnefs of the road, come reeking into the inn-yard, and nearly ex-piring under the extreme exertion to which he has been driven ! his fides bleeding with the fpurs or lafhes

lashes of the unfeeling post-boys!
every muscle and tendon quivering
with convulsive agony! In vain is
he offered food; his mouth is parched
with thirst and dust, he refuses sus-
tenance, water he is denied, because
it would probably put an end to his
existence, and he is preserved for
future and constant torment. But
there must be some great cause, a
stranger would say, some very good
reason, why horses have been driven
so unmercifully. On the contrary,
it is the constant custom of those,
who by their situations can afford
it, to tip the postillion an extraor-
dinary gratuity, for which sum he
would, at any time, flog his horses,
who must suffer in proportion, till
they

they nearly expire under the torture. Inhuman cuftom! barbarous polite-nefs! dreadful effect of *polifhed* man-ners! I have myfelf no doubt, that we muft inevitably hereafter give an account of the expenditure of our time, and the motives upon which we acted, and that thofe who thus unfeelingly indulge them-felves in fuch procedures towards the brutal creation, when no caufe of moment demands fuch exertions, will be called upon to anfwer for thofe mercilefs lafhes, and for thofe excruciating pangs, wantonly in-flicted upon the uncomplaining ani-mals, by whom they are fo fwiftly drawn.

THESE

THESE poor creatures, alas! experience no advantage from the prohibition contained in the fourth commandment; but, by the force of all-ruling fashion, are doomed to suffer more on that day than on any other. But shall not this double breach of the laws of Heaven and humanity meet with double retribution, in the future dispensation of rewards and punishments? While the gentleman turns with horror from the brutal carman, inflicting unmerited punishment on his faithful horses, let him reflect, that he is himself more culpable in the practice above-mentioned, because his education ought

to

to have inculcated better principles.

LET not thefe reflections be called
too ftrong, or too fevere—the caufe
of humanity (the *caufe* of every
thinking and *confiderate man*) demands
it. So various, fo complicated are
the evils under which the domeftic
animals fuffer by the hand of man,
that no expreffion can be too forcible
to refcue them from the cruelties
under which they fo often lan-
guifh.

IN the preface to this book, I
declared that I had no motive but
the good of mankind in view, when
I took

I took up my pen—the fame motive has conducted me through the
whole.—I have not the leaft idea
of perfonality, my aim alone being,
if poffible, to ftem the current of
vice and folly.

If I have deferved well of my
fellow - citizens, and fhould the
voice of the public applaud my
little labours, I fhall be amply gratified.

Should I have over-rated my
trifling abilities, I fhall ftill have
my motives for my confolation.
Unknown, and therefore concealed
from perfonal contempt, I fhall ever

make

make my own heart eafy, with the reflection, that as my fole object was the good of others, no felf-reproach can ever harrafs my bofom, or give me one moment's difquiet.

F I N I S.